Numerology 2024

The time has come to grow and acquire abundance and prosperity. Success is obtained by thinking and dreaming big. 2024 is a powerful year, where you will be able to obtain money, power, and success.

Alina A. Rubi and Angeline Rubi

Introduction

There is no such thing as chance, there is synchronicity. We are all born on a day, place, date, and time that are not a whim of fate. We bring specific missions and lessons from past lives.

By using numerology, we will have more autonomy and take control of our destiny.

Numerology is the study of numbers and their meaning. It is a discipline based on the concept that the name, day, month, and year of your birth contain fundamental information related to you. By analyzing the numerical values of the letters that make up your first and last name and the digits in your birth date, you can learn important aspects of your personality and your purpose in life.

Numerology is an ancient esoteric tradition that has been used by all mystics and philosophers for thousands of years in China, Greece, Rome, and Egypt.

Numerology is the correspondence between numbers and events, and the analysis of how they affect life. We can use Numerology to know ourselves and explore our talents. It is so broad that we can use it to acquire information about our health, professions, relationships, and purposes in life.

Pythagoras has been credited with being the first to master this tool, which is why he is considered the father of numerology. Not only did he make extensive contributions to the progress and perfection of numerology, but he is also the creator of multiple mathematical hypotheses.

Numerology 2024

*According to Numerology 2024 this year adds the number **8**.*

This number is related to abundance, power, balance, and justice.

During this 2024 we must reevaluate the way we relate to prosperity. We must be organized, pay our financial debts, and organize our lives more efficiently. It is a year where we must value our time and focus on the important things.

We must learn to live without fear, and we must try to heal our wounds on a subconscious level.

This year will give you the opportunity to be prosperous on a spiritual and material level. You must raise your self-esteem levels to achieve it.

It will be a year with many challenges, but you must remember that you will learn from them.

Worldwide there will be an increase in criticism and rebellions against abuses, tyrannies, violence, and dictatorships.

What does the number 2024 mean spiritually?

The meanings of the individual digits that make up the number 2024 according to numerology are:
The number 2 symbolizes duality, family, private and social life. You will enjoy your home life and family gatherings.

The number 2 indicates a sociable, friendly, and empathetic person. It is the number of cooperation, adaptability, and consideration for others.

This number symbolizes balance, union, and affinity. It is also an excellent mediator, honest and diplomatic. It represents intuition and vulnerability.

The number 4 comes to establish stability and evokes the sense of duty and discipline. It speaks to us of building solid foundations. This number teaches you to evolve in the material world, and to develop your logical mind.

The number 0 everything begins at the zero degree and at the zero point it ends. Sometimes we do not know the end, but we perceive the beginning, that is the zero point.

Tarot card according to the numerology 2024

The Strength.

Strength is the Tarot card 11 and 8 at the same time. This tarot card symbolizes firmness, strength, and tenacity to survive.

This arcanum represents the ability to overcome obstacles. The power of intelligence over strength. It is also the representation of patience, intuition, and reconciliation of opposites.

From the astrological point of view, the arcane of The Strength of the Tarot is related to the zodiac sign Leo and the planet Mars.

This tarot card numerologically has two perspectives, since it is number 11 in the Tarot de Marseille, a master number, and number 8 in the Rider Waite Tarot.

The Strength is the prototype of endurance. Always in touch with his intuition and creativity, but with a super-developed talent, liveliness, perception, and subtlety.

The Strength has the capacity to control the most essential instincts to achieve its purposes. It never surrenders, and it does not die out, it only resists.

The Strength unfailingly achieves what it sets out to do, overcoming every difficulty with perspicacity and cunning.

This arcane will test your capacity for endurance, fortitude, tolerance, your limits, and if you really want to change something, or achieve a goal, you will have to be persevering without giving up trying.
This means that to achieve your goals you will have to stop being impatient, banish fear, and bury your ego.

If last year you were trying to reach a goal and you couldn't reach it that means you were using the wrong methods. So, this year The Strength is asking you not to change the goal, but to change your attitude and the methods that are not working for you.

You must use the energies of the arcane The Strength to fill yourself with its courage and endurance. You must be stoic, daring, and determined, to conquer your fears, and you will achieve this only with discipline and perseverance.

Nothing will prevent you from reaching your goals, you should not rush, nor should you turn your back on the challenges that come your way.

This is an arcane of power, do not rush, embrace the challenges, and continue patiently. You possess the power and endurance to win. Don't feel bad about things that are out of your control, focus on you, on your inner self. You must polish yourself to become your best version.

In love, this tarot card signifies fidelity and stable relationships. It symbolizes the daily effort that every couple must make to maintain a healthy relationship, so that it becomes a happy union.

In the material aspect this tarot card announces that a prosperous season is coming, and that if you are smart you will be able to master any situation no matter how difficult it may be. You will receive all the recognition you deserve; you will be rewarded. This is the year to fulfill your dreams.

Your work capacity will increase, you will be persevering, and you will know how to plan and go the extra mile, always with your eyes on the future.

This tarot card announces that your health will be good, as you will have a lot of vitality. You will have to be disciplined around your well-being, but you are on the right track, you will be very healthy.

This Tarot card: **The Strength,** *reminds you that you have the capacity and inner strength to be able to achieve everything you set your mind to.*

Number of Life or Mission Trajectory

To calculate your Life Path or Mission number, that digit that shows you your skills and abilities, and gives you clues about the opportunities in your life, you must add up your birth date, that is, add up all the digits of your natal date.

For example, if a man named Juan Carlos Pau was born on December 7, 1965, his birth number is 4.

The breakdown of this procedure is as follows:

$7 + 1 + 2 + 1 + 9 + 6 + 5 = 31$

This is derived from the numerical place of the month in the year, which is 12, the numerical date in the month, which is 7, and the numerical breakdown of the year, which is 1, 9, 6 and 5.

Since 31 is a composite number, it is separated and added:

$3 + 1 = 4$

Therefore, Juan Carlos' life path number in this example is 4, a number that achieves his goals through a combination of his tenacious attitude, common sense, and love.

Meaning of the number 1

The number one represents unity. These people are characterized by their desire to do what they want and to impose those desires on the people around them. These people are very skillful, since apparently, they will make you believe that they accepted your opinion, but behind they are going to do what they want.

They are very energetic and rebellious people, but for the most part they are successful, regardless of their profession.

They want their life's achievements to leave a mark, and they are afraid that they will not achieve recognition at the professional and work level.

The number 1 represents the ability to adapt and react to anticipated and unforeseen changes.

It symbolizes leadership and generosity at its best. They are intelligent and extroverted people. They have a strong personality and are prone to be a bit selfish.

People with this number live life with intensity, without limitations. They have no ethical problems and behave passionately without worries.

These people, when they believe in an idea or cause, defend it to the end. Their convictions are so deep that they are willing to fight hard to protect what they believe is right.

They are determined people, when they set a goal they achieve it, even if they encounter millions of obstacles in their way. They are not afraid to sacrifice.

They are very friendly, have a great sense of humor. They are usually popular and are a pleasure to be around.

They are sensitive to offenses, but do not take seriously the offenses they themselves make. If someone hurts them deeply, they will not hesitate to take revenge and will become cruel individuals.

Their mission in life is not only to accomplish their own goals, but to help others accomplish them as well. They possess the ability to motivate others.

The challenge for people with this number is to not be so focused on themselves and to contaminate those around them with their enthusiasm to spur them into action.

They are very independent people, and if, due to certain life circumstances, they must depend on someone else, they will fall into depression.

Their aspiration in life is to be independent, and when they achieve it, they focus on being leaders.

No matter what area they work in, the number 1 will always lead and dictate the rules within their work or professional area.

Among the negative aspects of the number 1 are narcissism, self-centeredness, and irritation. Sometimes they run the risk of having uncontrolled ambition and of being haughty, vain, and impertinent.

People who are number 2 two are characterized by being protective, noble, and affable.

They like to receive people in their home and take care of them, that fills them with euphoria and pleasure. They are generous and generally have many friends.

They like to plan parties and will never forget the birthdays of friends and family, let alone their wedding anniversaries.

People with the number 2 are always involved in community activities or affiliated with political groups. These activities satisfy their need for recognition and allow them to enjoy being around other people.

The 2 is a considerate individual who is willing to help others. They like to feel wanted and needed.

The childhood of people with number 2 is good. They can give love. They are also very intuitive about other people's emotions; they know how to read other people's souls. They hate to be alone.

The typical number 2 always has a house full of friends and if unable to do so will resort to long conversations on the phone with friends and loved ones.

Social and family life is important to the number 2. They usually marry very young because of their desire to start a family, and usually have many children, becoming excellent parents.

Conflicts scare him, because they do not have a resilient spirit, nor a constant one.

They excel in their professional area, but it is difficult for them to achieve absolute success because they lack perseverance. They are also a bit lazy, although they would not admit it, not even to themselves.

If they fail, they look for excuses in external factors, but never make a constructive analysis about the particularities of their personality that triggered that failure.

Their aspiration is to capture the attention of those around them. To achieve this, they seduce those around them by supplying them with what they want. The problem is that they promise more than they can deliver.

They can become very permissive parents and raise wayward children.

They are attracted to caresses, they need to hug, kiss everyone they love, and they love to be kissed and hugged.

They excel in sports, especially group sports.

They have a connection with nature, so they frequently plan excursions with their family and friends.

If his financial resources allow it, the 2 will have a house in the countryside where he will be happy, in contact with nature and animals.

At work people with this number are those who work with the public and handling personnel.

Meaning of the number 3

The number 3 represents expansion. These people are characterized by their perspicacity to achieve everything they yearn for.

They are analytical people and study in detail all the information that comes into their hands to make the most of all opportunities.

They are persistent with their goals and will do whatever it takes to achieve them. However, the strength they put in at the beginning is extinguished when time goes by, and their objectives are not achieved. If this happens, they change projects.

If they want something and find a path that is shorter to where they want to go, they will take it, regardless of whether that path is morally right.

Many do not have the willpower and stamina to overcome the difficulties that may come their way.

Their feelings are volatile, one day they are thrilled, but a month later they may lose interest completely.

People with the number 3 are fascinated by always starting over.

If they maintain an interest in something, they will put all their mental capacity and skills into it, but they will not be able to maintain that interest for long.

The routine tires them out and when they change their interests, they become enthusiastic again.

In love, the same thing happens to them. Personality 3 is narcissistic, and it is difficult for them to maintain stable relationships.

They are seductive, cordial, charismatic and friendly. If they want to conquer someone, they will succeed because the person will not be able to resist their attractive methods of seduction.

They usually fall in love at first sight and feel that the person they have found is their soul mate.

They feel this way, and by the time they start the relationship they are already thinking about getting married and having children. Unfortunately, this doesn't happen because the infatuation fades away before they reach the altar.

They are prone to having two personalities. On the one hand, they try to preserve appearances, to appear confident to the world, and to take care of their image. On the other hand, they have inner insecurity and fear that someone might expose them.

They go by their intuition; if they hurt someone, a genuine apology will be no problem.

Meaning of the number 4

The number 4 symbolizes willpower. It is common for people with number 4 to confuse tenacity with stubbornness.

They tend to defend their opinions in front of others and will continue to defend it, even if the evidence proves them wrong.

They find it difficult to recognize when they are wrong and almost never assuming their mistakes.

The 4 is distinguished by their responsibility. At work, they are admirable thanks to this quality. If they must finish a job, they can stay up all night to have it done on time.

At work or in any other activity they perform, number 4 will have excellent attendance.

You will not miss any of your obligations for any reason, the only thing that could prevent you from doing so would be a serious illness.

At home and with their partner, number 4's are difficult people because they exaggerate situations and tend to drown in a glass of water. They create problems for trifles and that bothers a lot to their family circle. These bursts of bad temper do not last long, and number 4 quickly regains their composure and forgets about the incident.

They are optimistic and sarcastic, with great mental quickness and a sense of humor that amuses their friends.

They are analytical about the character of others and can spot flaws that people wish to hide. It is difficult to fool a number 4 and those who try are victims of their satire.

A number 4 is unlikely to attend a party and go unnoticed because their sense of humor and outgoing personality will make them the center of attention.

Among its negative aspects we can find that the number 4 usually has moments of sadness, during which it focuses its energies negatively.

He usually dedicates these melancholic moments to analyze his life, but due to his state of mind and lack of enthusiasm he ends up dissatisfied with himself and his life.

These moments are of solitude, and he does not discuss his reflections with anyone. He likes to show himself as a confident and optimistic person and to hide his insecurities.

Meaning of the number 5

In numerology the number 5 is known as the expert hermit.

People with this number think of life as an exciting adventure.

They are analytical and logical and like to discover the mysteries of everything that happens around them. Ignorance and lack of knowledge bother them.

Intelligence for them is the best virtue. They are brilliant and they know it, for that reason they are a little arrogant, curious and will seek to increase their knowledge.

They are usually melancholic and introverted people. However, they are good at listening to others and giving advice.

Their goal in life is to learn and money for the number 5 is only a means for them to travel or to buy time to be able to dedicate themselves quietly to study the subjects that interest them. Getting rich is never their goal and their energies will be focused on something higher.

They are not very communicative, sometimes even their closest friends often consider them an unknown quantity. For a number 5 it is important to protect their privacy, and to keep an emotional distance from others as it makes them feel protected. Incidentally, they isolate themselves from the people who form their core.

Number 5's are intellectual people, but they can also dedicate themselves to religious life.

Some are introverted and enjoy solitude like no other number. They abhor feeling tormented and like their privacy to be respected.

They are homebodies and always establish strong and lasting bonds of friendship but will not have such an active social life.

They have an incredible imagination and intellectual capacity. They like to make the most of their time because for them, fun is a way of wasting it. If it were up to them, they would dedicate every minute of their lives to study.

The number 5 has a need for affection and to feel loved, but they do not know how to ask for it, nor how to approach other people. They are disconnected from their emotions, and their own feelings are alien to them, as if it were someone else who is feeling them.

They tend to be selfish with money, but this does not mean that they are eager to accumulate wealth, but rather that they prefer to manage their resources to have peace of mind and to be able to devote their intellectual capacity to matters that truly interest them.

When someone offends a number 5, he will not respond with insults or fights, but if the offense is great, the number 5 number will withdraw the affection he feels towards his aggressor. When the number 5 loses appreciation towards someone it is forever. They are implacable and unforgiving.

Meaning of the number 6

People with the number 6 show a peaceful countenance to the outside world. This is only a facade because inside they are often tormented by existential problems and fears.

They persistently feel a sense of danger, which may really exist or be just a figment of their imagination. They may feel a deep fear of change, mistakes, loneliness, and betrayal.

They suffer from insecurity and lack of self-confidence. They believe they are not capable of dealing with conflict situations and this terrifies them.

They communicate well socially despite their shyness. However, they tend to feel watched and persecuted, so they do not trust anyone. They doubt people's intentions, and sometimes this attitude causes them to isolate themselves.

People with the number 6 hate confusions linked to the sentimental area, they say what they feel clearly and expect the same from their partners. They try too hard to be kind and polite.

The number 5 has a dual personality, its inner world is totally different from the world it shows to the outside.

The number 6 has difficulty in knowing themselves, they are unstable and will go from exaggerated optimism to dramatic pessimism, they do not know how to find balance.

In their relationships they fluctuate from one extreme to the other; if they meet someone they like, they immediately consider him or her the best friend in the world. However, they eventually become disillusioned and move away from that person.

During childhood people with the number 6 have felt fear towards people in authority, most were raised by possessive people who amplified in the number 6 that insecurity.

As adults, they try to counteract this feeling of insecurity by forming a sentimental relationship with a person who can make them feel emotionally protected.

When it comes to deciding, number 6 is reluctant to give his opinion or to decide on any subject. If he is forced to give his opinion, he will hardly show what he really feels unless he is with people he trusts.

At work they are energetic and efficient. They could concentrate.

They can be promoted and occupy important positions because they are detail-oriented and persevering.

They can work as part of a team and follow orders smoothly.

They are considerate of their family members and easily show their affection.

Meaning of the number 7

The number 7 is the most spiritual number. These people possess an enormous intuitive capacity.

What torments them is the feeling that they are not taking advantage of life. They need to live permanently new experiences, through which they can learn and incorporate knowledge. They love to travel, to know other cultures, to learn new languages and will do everything possible to satisfy their desire for adventure.

Generally, people with the number 7 have had a childhood in which they were intellectually stimulated, learned to think for themselves and have very sound judgment.

They like to relate to people and establish permanent bonds. Friendship for the number 7 is a serious matter, he has few friends, but he keeps his friendships for life.

They are supportive and compassionate. They are empathetic and put themselves in the other's place.

Generally, they are involved in some charitable activity.

It is not easy to deceive a number 7 due to their intuition they detect without difficulty the evil, falsehood and bad intentions. They choose well the people in their inner circle, they like altruistic people and stay away from insensitive and selfish people. This attitude has earned them the reputation of being arrogant.

They like the balance between their social life and time alone to reflect on their circumstances.

The number 7 is utopian; they start activities that they never finish or make plans that they never carry out. As a result, they are likely to suffer from pessimism.

They are guided by their intuition. They are extroverted and fun. Loneliness will never agree with number 7 and causes changes in their temperament.

All number 7s are characterized by being studious and introspective. They like to analyze knowledge and adopt new perspectives on the subjects they discover.

They are passionate about intellectual debates, where they can defend their points of view and at the same time listen to the opinions of others.

During their childhood, the number 7 was educated to know how to overcome fears by using their imagination. It is common for people with this number not to have had a good relationship with their parents and to have rebelled against parental authority. When they want to, they can be completely charming and win the sympathy of anyone.

Meaning of the number 8

People with the number 8 are characterized by being very sensitive. Because of this sensitivity they are impressionable. They should be treated with delicacy since they can be easily hurt.

In the social area they shine due to their sympathy, charisma, and quickness of mind. They are attractive because of their manners and education.

They are somewhat harsh in judging others. They tend to be sympathetic with their mistakes, but rigid and demanding with the mistakes of others.

They do not accept that anyone point out their mistakes, and they hardly let the mistakes of others go unnoticed. Indulgence is legitimate only for themselves. They can be a bit cruel.

The number 8 generally has a very high self-concept and shows it through sarcastic comments.

At work they are not good at teamwork, they are rebellious and generate a lot of conflicts. They are prone to self-pity and to think that they are the most unhappy and unfortunate people on the planet.

They are very inconsistent in mood, one day they can be very interested in something or someone, and the next day they can completely lose their interest. In love they can be very affectionate one moment, and the next they can be totally indifferent. They like their wishes to be fulfilled and to achieve this they use their words, as they are excellent speakers and convince anyone with ease.

Their behavior varies according to their convenience. They are rebellious without a cause, and do not like to follow orders. However, if it suits them, they will behave like the most docile people in the world.

Money lovers, the number 8 lives comfortably, without economic problems. They are thrifty and good managers.

If someone hurts them, which is easy, they become vengeful and do not stop until they feel they have been repaid in kind. However, with people they trust they are sensitive and are always ready to help their loved ones.

Number 8's are not melancholic people and much less reflective. They like to enjoy the pleasures of life without any philosophical or existential problems. They usually have a cheerful character when relating to others.

Meaning of the number 9

People with the number 9 are mentally independent and suffer if they feel coerced.

Their personality is super optimistic, they manage to find a positive side to everything, regardless of the drama of any situation.

They are direct and honest, and if they have personnel in their charge, they make impartial decisions. This characteristic quickly earns them the esteem of their subordinates.

They hate betrayal, if they betrayed someone, they would never forgive them. They are people who know how to say things so as not to hurt anyone. Socially, they are distinguished by their brilliant answers.

They are observant and detail oriented. They know who to trust and who not to trust, although they will never treat anyone badly.

They are never in a bad mood; their character is cheerful and that is why everyone wants to be by their side.

The sin of the number 9 is laziness. They are not active; they like to sleep and rest without doing anything. They are not suspicious and are easily influenced by others.
They are not very clear about their objectives and therefore let themselves be carried away by the ideas of others. Sometimes they are irresponsible, they get carried away by emotions and do not think about the consequences.

They are usually lucky, but through negligence they miss opportunities that other numbers would instantly take advantage of.
They are afraid of difficulties, run away from them when they arise and do not have the capacity to resist complicated situations.

In love the number 9 may tend to exaggerate feelings, but it is passionate.

The pessimism of the people around them does not affect them since their optimism resists any situation. They are not rancorous; they quickly forget offenses. They have a noble heart and soul.

They are generous and are always willing to justify the defects of others, they are not demanding with others.

They often give up their own desires to conform to the expectations others have of them. They are not fighters, so they tend to give up easily.

How to Calculate Your Destination or Expression Number

Your Fate or Expression number is calculated based on your first and last name. This number shows your talents, gifts, and weaknesses.

It is calculated with your full name, if you have two names you must use them, and you must avoid abbreviations. You must assign a number to each letter of your name using the following table:

1 - A, J, S

2 - B, K, T

3 - C, L, U

4 - D, M, V

5 - E, N, W

6 - F, O, X

7 - G, P, Y

8 - H, Q, Z

9 - I, R

Note: *For the following letters: "CH" uses C = 3 and H = 8. "LL" as two L's, i.e., 3-3 and "Ñ" is 5, as N*

Once you have identified the numbers that correspond to each letter of your name, you must add them together and reduce them to a single digit.

Remember to include the last names. The only numbers you cannot reduce are 11 and 22, because they are master numbers.

After you have converted your first and last name to a single digit, you must add them together and reduce them to a single digit. That will be your expression number.

For our friend Juan Carlos Pau, it would be as follows:

1+3+1+5+3+1+9+3+6+1+7+1+3 = 44

27 is a composite number and must be simplified:

4 + 4 = 8

Juan Carlos Pau's expression number is 8.

Meanings of Destination or Expression Numbers

Expression or Destination Number 1

You are independent and passionate. You can influence the emotions of the people around you. You are the number one, therefore, you are a leader par excellence because you possess a magnetic aura of authority. Those who possess this expression number are sometimes vain and conceited, their identity is intense, and when others are not in tune with their interests or do not live up to their expectations, they sink into pessimism and melancholy.

Expression Number or Destination 2

They are careless, negligent, and apathetic. They possess a sharp instinct. They are generous and rude words annoy them. They become irritable and upset when confronted with conflict. They are sociable and love their friends.

Expression or Destination Number 3

They are spiritual dreamers, generous, expressive, and enthusiastic. They could influence the people around them. They are friendly, have excellent intelligence and ability to express themselves, and face conflicts with courage and creativity.

Expression or Destination Number 4

These people are organized and resolve conflicts methodically. They love music and art. They enjoy when they are in a relationship, for them love is the most sublime thing in the universe. You can trust them with your eyes closed, but sometimes they are very stubborn and implacable.

Expression or Destination Number 5

These people love transformation, enjoy being independent, and are always looking for new experiences and challenges. They take advantage of circumstances and enjoy life to the fullest. Sometimes they are careless and make mistakes, but because they are so skilled, they get out of challenges quickly.

Expression Number or Destination 6

They are charming, kind, sympathetic, and empathetic people. Sometimes they tend to care more for others than for themselves. They are honest and lawful. They are very fair people. They possess the ability to heal and are creative.

Expression or Destination Number 7

They are intelligent, witty, insightful, and with a great zest for life that leads them to inquire into all known and unknown areas. They are discreet with their thoughts and inclinations. Some are skeptical, and solitary.

Number of Expression or Destination 8

These people possess incredible potential. When they set a goal they achieve it, as they are aggressive with their aspirations. Abundance, well-being, happiness, and fortune are always present in their lives.

Expression or Destination Number 9

People with this number have amazing focus and humanity. Their interests and perspectives are always aimed at bringing about changes that will benefit the world at large. They do not like to judge because they believe that all souls have a spark of goodness and love within them.

Expression or Destination Master Numbers

Expression or Destination Number 11

People with this number are old souls who have lived countless incarnations. They are passionate about everything they do. They are sensitive to their environment, so they must protect themselves from black magic or negative energies.

Expression or Destination Number 22

Your capabilities make you trustworthy. This number represents those people who understand that we come to this planet to evolve. They are easily frustrated by the lack of values of human beings.

Expression or Destination Number 33

They are strict, but affectionate people. They are leaders from birth. They have a magnetic aura that you can feel when you are in their presence. They can take on big projects, no matter how difficult they are. They are always willing to help anyone in need, avoid conflict and love peace. They do not like to mix with aggressive people because their personality is peaceful. They could persuade.

Karmic Debt Numbers

The karmic debt numbers contain a high concentration of karmic events from the past, and these results are still being felt in these lifetimes. It is helpful to know how these people are harmed by these numbers, and how they can overcome these challenges. These numbers can damage vibrations as the spiritual and karmic debris they contain are uniquely expressed.

***The numbers of karmic debts are 13, 14, 16 and 19** and whenever they appear in the results before simplifying a final amount, you should pay close attention because of the harmful effects they can cause.*

People with karmic debt numbers are blessed and chosen people, because when they overcome these challenges they evolve differently, they acquire spiritual powers and that differentiates them from others.

Karmic Debt Number 13
These people should not be disillusioned, since frustrations, disappointments, disappointments, and losses are the basis of their learning.

People with karmic debt number 13 face many obstacles and countless failures because of their self-centered actions of the past.

To succeed the karmic debt number 13 must be persevering, fight for his dreams, have discipline and never go down unethical paths to succeed.

Karmic Debt Number 14

*People with **karmic debt number** 14 spend most of their lives in crisis, these crises depress them, but they can overcome them if they use their mental strength.*

These people attract many challenges. They misused their power and freedom in other lives, so in this life they find themselves in the mire of sex, drugs, and alcohol. They are prone to indulge in vices and abuse their free will negatively. If they exercise control and are disciplined, they can achieve their goals. They must be organized and committed to get what they want.

Karmic Debt Number 16

These people pursue things that are not meant for them and spend a long time at it. When they fail, they feel miserable because these goals were not a waste of time and a meaningless struggle. People karmic debt number 16 through are chained to delusions and illusions. They must use these challenges as points of metamorphosis. They should calm their uneasy and worried minds, come out of their world of illusions, and try to be humble.

Karmic Debt Number 19

These people will face multiple separations. This could be in their circles of friends, loved ones or separations from their goals. These people should try not to isolate themselves.

People with **karmic debt number** *19 are forced to be independent since childhood, this independence makes them believe that being independent is a requirement. As adults, they strive to be alone and refuse any help.*

The phenomenon of seeing repeated numbers.

It is a reality that we are surrounded by numbers, and in contact with them every second, but there are times when we feel that there are certain numbers that haunt us, wherever we look we see them repeated: on watches, computers, car license plates, television, shopping receipts and even in dreams. There is no such thing as coincidence, there is synchronicity, and this phenomenon is called numerical synchronicity.

Perhaps in the past this was a rarity, but every day more and more people are witnessing this phenomenon happening to them, and many are questioning the established models to try to find a valid answer for them.

Specialists in the field authenticate that this mystery along with a higher global consciousness is creating new sensations, causing many people to evolve spiritually. This manifestation of seeing numbers repeatedly can also be categorized as a sign. Almost all of us have numbers that we consider lucky or preferred and it can happen that we suddenly see this number everywhere. When receiving this type of message, most of the time hidden to our own eyes, but not to our mind, it shows that we can perceive other realities.

From ancient to modern times, the sacred science of numerology has maintained its notability. Numbers teach opportunities for growth, life teachings and instruction within each experience.

Some people see numerical sequences of particular significant events. But the most common numerical patterns are 11:11, 222 and 333. All these numbers, according to astrology and numerology, are master numbers with a unique meaning, representing different aspects of the inner self, from personality to spirituality, these numbers influence more than others and therefore captivate our attention.

11:11 - Watch your thoughts carefully and be sure to think only of what you want, not what you don't want. This sequence is a sign that there is an opportunity opening, and your thoughts are materializing very quickly.

222 - Our newly planted ideas are beginning to come to fruition. Keep nurturing them and they will soon manifest. In other words, don't give up five minutes before the miracle happens.

333 - The ascended masters are close to you, wanting you to know that you have their help, love, and companionship. Call on the ascended masters often, especially when you see patterns with the number 3 forming around you.

These figures increase awareness and perception because they offer us a channel to the subconscious.

This phenomenon happens unexpectedly, but at the exact moment and occurs for a reason, sometimes changing the direction of our lives and influencing our thoughts. When the universe has a message for us, this is one of the ways to get our attention. We must remain receptive to the world around us because numbers are the language of nature and everything around us can be represented by numbers.

"Everything in the Universe is mathematically precise and each number has its own energy, vibration and meaning. The placement of numbers in a sequence has a special meaning." Pythagoras

Numerology for Babies Born in the Year 2024

Babies Number 1
They will be a child with leadership skills. They will have an innate ability to negotiate, control and manage people and projects.

Babies Number 2
They will be calculating and powerful children. They will have a positive attitude towards life's challenges, and a lot of self-confidence.

Babies Number 3
They will be very equitable, reasonable, and serene children.
These children will always stand up for just causes. They will be very perceptive and have a heightened state of awareness.

Babies Number 4
They will be children who will always be looking for challenges, they will not be afraid of obstacles because these setbacks will make them stronger.

Babies Number 5
They will be children with financial skills, they will not be materialistic. They will have excellent money management and business skills. They may have an ability for mathematics.

Babies Number 6

They will be children who will struggle to maintain a balance between the material and spiritual world. They will always try to maintain harmony between their work, social and personal life.

Babies Number 7

They will be responsible and giving children. These children will be intelligent, they would like to help others. They will also be very spiritual.

Babies Number 8

These children will be very stable and self-controlled. They will be organized, stable and very prosperous.

Babies Number 9

*They will be strong-willed children.
Very hard-working and goal oriented. They will be independent and with an incredible power of determination.*

Definition of the Personal Year

Probably every time a year begins you ask yourself questions and write down goals without knowing what challenges the new year holds for you.

When a year begins, a chapter in our lives closes, but a cycle begins that challenges us because we are not sure if all our dreams can come true.

What's in store for me in the New Year? Will I buy a house, get a new partner, change jobs? Is this the right year to have children?

It is important to have an open mind when we are so uncertain about things that are new or different. But with numerology we can use our personal year and get an idea of how things may be.

The Universal Year Numbers are different from the others, because they do not depend on your name and date of birth. The first two digits of the Year Number represent the balance of that century. The third digit of the Year Number symbolizes the rhythm of the decade. The fourth digit has no specific meaning.

How to calculate your Personal Year.

This is an example:

Juan Carlos was born on December 7, 1965.

To know your personal year 2024, we make this calculation:

7 (day of birth) + 1+2 (month of birth) + 2 + 0 + 2 + 2 + 4(starting year) = 18 (1 + 8) = 9

For Juan Carlos, the year 2024 is a Personal Year 9.

This number is important, specifically if the result is one of the master numbers: 11, 22, 33.

The personal year describes what you must do during this period. They will be options, changes, or reinforcements that will enrich your path.

Year Staff 1

Key words for Year 1*: Transformation, Research, Engagement.*

A new chapter in your life begins. You're likely to move, get a new job or meet new people who will change your life forever.

This year you will lay the groundwork for new projects and ideas. It is a stage where you will be reborn. You should consider this year as the perfect time to change different aspects of your life, there are things that no longer work for you, and you must let them go.

This year offers you the invitation to take courage and try to fulfill your dreams, you will really have enthusiasm to make changes. Take courage and explore new opportunities and attitudes that will help you change the focus of your life.

This year 2024 is a personal invitation to trust, reflect on what you want, choose objectively, and decide what you want to succeed in. Try to choose what really makes you happy.

Start by cataloging the things you want to change, including improvements in your daily life, such as changing your eating habits or exercising. Remember that to start something you must plan it with consistency and determination.

This year is the perfect opportunity to close a cycle, you must leave behind everything that is not useful to you. Concentrate on what will help you grow, develop, or learn. Do not be afraid to let go of what was useful in the past.

You need to forget the past and look to the future. Too many things have happened that may have confused your mind, those things prevent you from accessing the paths that lead to happiness.

If you have businesses and projects, strive to keep them growing without forcing things. Try to give everything a rhythm.

Try not to acquire new debts.

Life will reward you.

Personal Year 2

Key words for Year 2: *Responsibility, Harmony, Stability.*

This year you should continue to build. The year 2024 will allow you to meet tutors, teachers, or even a partner. The energies of the year focus on cooperation and patience.

You start a development phase, and you must put your initiatives into practice. This year 2 may seem slow, but it is a period of defining your objectives.

You will probably encounter obstacles or people who try to limit your path, so it is important not to get overwhelmed and anxious. You should not worry about the things that are hindering your initiatives, it is just the natural settling in, and it is part of your growth process.

You must learn to be more diplomatic and tactful. People may appear willing to distract you, but that should not limit you from making new friends.

If when you did the calculation, the sum was 11, it means that you have reached your moment to breathe, to evolve and to become conscious.

The year of blessings is upon you. Try to get rid of all toxic people if you want to have a prosperous year, do not trust anyone.

The year 2024 offers you the opportunity to let go of your past worries and take charge of your life with more enthusiasm.

Life will present you with completely new plans and give you the opportunity to build your future if you leave the past behind. It is the year to think about yourself, break limits and not self-sabotage.

You must have courage and face life from a positive approach.

Personal Year 3

Key words for Year 3: Agility, Creativity, Information.

This is the year for you to look for ways to share your wisdom with the world. You will feel part of a greater whole and you will have much satisfaction and fulfillment.

You need to get rid of the feelings of restriction that you have accumulated. The only way to get results this year is to allow your creativity to express itself. Let go of rigidity, let your imagination be free. You must go the extra mile.

Find a new hobby, change your habits, start implementing new ideas and solutions to the challenges you face along the way.

You will have to work very hard, but you could strengthen your individual bonds, and form more formal relationships. These ties will be tested, certain relationships do not suit you. Perhaps they give you a lot of fun but have a dark side. Try to establish common goals with the people you love.

During this year you should be more conscious with your nutrition, and rest as your energy levels will be low.

Personal Year 4

Key words for Year 4: *Renewal, Restoration, Innovation, Assertiveness.*

This year you must work hard and be organized. If you manage to stay in the present, you can get to where you want to be.
Now is the time for you to reflect and analyze your personal goals. You need to establish a plan so that you can achieve something specific and well-structured.
Try to think about your future, try to assume all responsibilities and organize all your projects carefully. You may be a little self-critical and this may result in you establishing your views strongly, being more determined and fighting. This is positive as it will allow you to notice all the changes that occur in your environment.
All the above will inevitably have a positive effect on your family relationships and close friendships. you will be more assertive, and this will have a positive impact on your personal relationships.
If you organize yourself, this will be a year of prosperity, abundance, and triumphs. Trust in yourself because you will be able to recover your enthusiasm and live with illusion.

Inertia is your worst enemy this year, as well as negative thoughts. Destiny offers you the opportunity to achieve everything you yearn for, dare to fight for those dreams.

Personal Year 5

Key words for Year 5*: Character, Will, Effort, Courage, Courage, Ratification, Recognition, Visualization.*

A year where you will enjoy many adventures, emotions and where you will have the opportunity to plant seeds with the intention to succeed.

Year 5 for you is like an injection of enthusiasm, plan because it is a year of many changes. You must be prepared for some unforeseen circumstances. Try to be receptive to all opportunities and to all challenges.

You must have mental clarity, be cautious and never underestimate your potential.

Try to expand your circle of friends, keep your public image healthy, and pay close attention to the contracts you must sign.

Take care of yourself because this way you will have the success you deserve. Establish habits that will allow you to ensure your prosperity for years to come. Calculate the risks and decide on the perfect opportunities when they present themselves to you.

Don't rush and act wisely, always thinking about what is best for you in the long term. Forget about immediate results and accept that things take time, and you can't always expect them to happen when you want them to.

Personal Year 6

Key words for Year 6: *Reorganize, Reborn Reform, Replace, Manifest, Disseminate, Transmit, Inform, Participate.*

This year 2024 offers you the opportunity to heal sentimental wounds and to free yourself from all the repressed emotions that sleep in your subconscious.

You will be very focused on your home and family. It is the perfect time to create a more stable and harmonious environment in your surroundings.

It is key that this year you learn to share all that you have received in abundance. It is also necessary that you avoid impulsive actions so that you do not make mistakes.

Always act ethically, try to stay calm and be confident in your decisions. You will see incredible results and it will all be thanks to your courage. Everything that was paralyzed will suddenly begin to flow and you will feel liberated. Perhaps in some periods you will notice instability, but this is necessary for you to break the routine.
You will have opportunities to travel, enjoy and control excesses of any kind.

Personal Year 7

Key words for Year 7*: Investigation, Observation, Verification, Control, Transformations, Metamorphosis.*

During this year you will have many changes. These changes may be related to your friendships, relationships, work, and home.
There is a possibility that you will meet someone important who will help you advance in your profession or perhaps you will become engaged.

This is a "parenthesis" year as you will stop to value everything you have done. You must let go of everything that is not working, be it objects or relationships.
For this you must perfect your analytical skills and not be afraid to calmly make a thorough review of what limits you.

Due to these purification processes, your relationships will be debated. Through comparison you eliminate mistakes and errors.

You will be attracted to esoteric subjects, but you will grow spiritually. Don't forget that everyone comes to this life with a different contract than you and that you should not judge the path of others. Everyone is where he or she is meant to be.

Personal Year 8

Keywords for Year 8: *Success, Evolution, Restoration, Transformation, Rehabilitation, Reconstruction, Prosperity.*

Much abundance and success on your way. You will feel blessed by all the opportunities that will come your way. This personal year is related to karma, so if you have acted well, dividends await you. It will be an important year where you will be very busy.

This year you must put each piece in its place. It is time to make decisions, reflect, and choose what and who you want for your life.

You will feel more confident and will have more mental capacity to face challenges. You should take risks and begin studies that will help you to advance in your profession.
You will want to enjoy moments of solitude, accompanied by your thoughts, far away from the hustle and bustle of social networks. You should practice meditation combined with breathing techniques.
Do not give so much importance to superfluous matters, and toxic people.

Personal Year 9

__Key words for Year 9__: Overcome, Finish, Conclude, Accomplish, Perceive, Perceive, be instructed, be trained, Study, Experience, Deepen.

This year will be difficult if you resist change. It is a year of endings. Throw out what is useless and stay away from energy vampires.

Surround yourself with people who bring you knowledge and good energy. Protect yourself from black magic. Organize your house, throw away what you do not use, broken things, because in this way you will be making space for the new.

You must decide what you really want to do in your life, destiny will scream in your ears what you really want and if you are willing to fight for it.

The commitment this year is with yourself, you must. give up your fears and insecurities because during this period you should be attentive and not complain so much.

Your Soul Number. How to calculate it

Your soul number manifests your desires, satisfactions, hobbies, concerns, worries, and discomforts.

The soul is the spiritual part that we all have. Together with the mind and the body, the soul makes up the human being. In numerology, the soul is related to a number called: soul number.

This number comes from the vowels of the birth name and represents the inner self.

If you wish to calculate your soul number, you must identify the vowels of your full name. Do not forget to include middle names.

*You must use the vowels **A, E, I, O U**. If by chance your name has a Y, since the Y performs the function of a vowel you must use it. Examples are the names: Daryl, Dylan, Henry, **and** Taylor.*

The numerical value of each vowel is as follows:
A = 1
E = 5
I= 9
O = 6
U = 3
Y = 7

When you have identified the number of each vowel in your full name, the next step is to add them all up and reduce them to a single digit, except for the numbers 11 or 22, which are master numbers.

Meaning of the Soul Number

Number 1:
Independent souls who can take good care of themselves, have a clear vision of life goals and purposes.

Number 2:
Loving, artistic, calm, peaceful and polite, these are the soul's number 2. They also have a great imagination and creativity.

Number 3:
They are strong, determined, courageous, compassionate, enthusiastic, and very optimistic. They constantly think about the future.

Number 4:
They are obsessed with order, stability, and control. They are often frustrated when things don't go according to plan.

Number 5:

They are free, traveling souls who enjoy meeting new people. Challenges excite them and they are considered a leader soul.

Number 6:

Love is their most powerful soul, so they tend to prioritize the interests of others over their own. They are very balanced and full of harmony.

Number 7:

They live in a constant mental analysis of what they want from the world and life in general. They are very talented artists and not at all ambitious.

Number 8:

They are leading souls or figures in society, they aspire to be rich and have power and high status. Their ambition makes them the best at what they do. Number 9: It is the most selfless and dreamy soul. It is charismatic, understanding, and makes the world a better place.

Number 11:

They are creative, artistic, and charismatic. They possess a psychic side due to being one of the most sensitive souls.

Number 22:
It is a soul closely related to the 4 (2+2=4), but adds
the characteristics of honesty, kindness, and attention
to detail.

How to Calculate your Personal House Number

Your house number offers you the secrets to take advantage of its energetic vibrations. The home is our sanctuary, where our dreams, our family, and our ideas live. All these things are our treasures, that's why we must take care of the energetic flow that surrounds us, specifically inside our home.

The decoration, the colors with which we paint our house influence the harmony, but they are not the only ones to consider. The address of your house offers predictive information according to numerology.

Steps to Calculate your Personal House Number

To know your personal home number, you must add up all the numbers that make up your address until you have a single digit.

Example*: If you live in the number 2550, you must add **2+5+5+5+0= 12**
1+2= 3*

If your address has letters included, you must look in the alphabetical table and change those letters to numbers.

1 (A, J, S)
2 (B, K, T)
3 (C, L, U)
4 (D, M, V)
5 (E, N, W)
6 (F, O, X)
7 (G, P, Y)
8 (H, Q, Z)
9 (I, R)

If you lived in a building with the number 2550, in apartment 8F, you must add up all the numbers and letters.

*Example: **2+5+5+0+8+6 (6 is the letter F) = 26** **2+6=8.***

The 8 will be the number that corresponds to this house.
Remember that if there were letters in the address it would be another number because you would have to add those numerical values to the previous one.

Meaning of your House number

Number 1

You must be very attentive to the type of energies that enter your house because the people who visit you leave bad energies inside your home. With neighbors you should be careful because they are very envious, they are curious about who enters and leaves your house, and those bad eyes create an energetic imbalance.

Number 2

It indicates that the happiness of your house does not lie in its luxury, but in the harmony that you are able to maintain inside it. This house will make you forget the chaos that exists in the world. The way you communicate, the words you say are important because houses are containers of energies. Everything is engraved on the walls. There is the possibility of accidents inside.

Number 3

*This house number means enthusiasm, optimism, happiness. In these houses the energy is in constant movement. In this house you will be able to achieve your goals and be successful. **The number 3 attracts*** *good luck, for that reason in this house people will always be undertaking new projects.*

Number 4

If your house has this number, you will not live in it for long, let's say it is a transit house. It is a house for new beginnings, here you can start your family, but guaranteed that when it grows you will move. If you stay here for a long time, discrepancies, disagreements, contradictions, antagonisms, hostilities, and inconsistencies will constantly arise.

Number 5

In this house there will always be parties or family gatherings. You may not have to do much structural work, but there will always be a lot of tension inside the house because of all the people who visit it. In this house there will never be two similar days. Its owners will be very diverse, but if you like it and you don't want to move, you must be constantly cleaning it energetically.

Number 6

This house always has good vibes, that's why you should keep it illuminated. It is the perfect home for newly married couples starting a life project. Here the family will have the necessary conditions to live in peace. It will also make the people who live here compassionate.

Number 7

This is the ideal house for artists as it has favorable conditions for creativity and reflection. Its inhabitants will be very spiritual. For writers and students, it would be the perfect one. It is advisable to check periodically if the house has escapes of energies or concentration of bad vibrations.

Number 8

This number is related to wealth; however, it is not the appropriate place to form and maintain a family, nor to live happily with your partner. **In this house everyone will be constantly concerned only with money and** *material* **things.** *This can create tension in the home. For a workplace it is perfect.*

Number 9

In this house people can become a bit dull and vague, although within this house there will be balance, fairness, equality, and empathy. This would be the ideal house for a social worker, or a lawyer. It possesses healing energies.

Numerology and Health Care

Your personal number reveals your health weaknesses and how to strengthen it.

The sum of your date of birth and its reduction to a single digit result in your personal number. In the previous pages you have how to calculate it.

This number reveals to your different particularities such as your mission in life, your character, and the weaknesses of your health, as well as how we should strengthen them. Numbers have energetic vibrations linked to people and influence your life.

When calculating your corresponding number, look for your weaknesses and how you can strengthen them.

Number 1

These people can be workaholics and for that reason it is common for them to be tired all the time. This fatigue manifests itself in the shoulders, knees, back and high blood pressure. These people need to exercise daily and avoid stressful situations.

Number 2

These people are prone to joint pain, migraine, and digestive system problems. These conditions are a consequence of repressing emotions. It is recommended that they express what they think and do not harbor any resentment.

Number 3

These people live their emotions to the extreme, that's why they suffer from weight, throat, and intestinal problems. Exercise is the perfect medicine to release all the stress.

Number 4

They often suffer from neuralgia, arthritis, and depression. It is important that they maintain a healthy diet and give priority to rest.

Number 5

These individuals are prone to addictions. They may have adrenal gland problems and osteoarthritis. Exercise, proper hydration, and healthy nutrition is the solution.

Number 6

These people want to control everything, for this reason they almost always suffer from headaches. They may also suffer from reproductive system problems. The consumption of sweets and dairy products in excess should be avoided. Stress makes them worse.

Number 7

These people suffer from insomnia, headaches and are prone to depression. They should avoid consuming processed foods and a lot of carbohydrates. It is recommended that they walk outdoors.

Number 8

These people worry excessively about material and economic things. For that reason, they are prone to heart problems, hypertension, and panic attacks. The solution is to enjoy life a little more. There has never been a happy millionaire in a hospital. They should laugh, have pets, and share with friends and family.

Number 9

These people suffer from neck pain, cardiovascular problems, anemia, and a weak immune system. Practicing yoga, breathing exercises and meditation are the best medicines.

Numerology and your Profession

Sometimes we have a job that we do because we have no other choice. However, even if you do not believe it, there is a job that would motivate you to want to be doing it constantly and with a lot of satisfaction.

Through numerology, with your personal number (remember that in the previous pages is how to calculate it) you can find professions that match your number and find a nice and favorable job.

Favorable professions for numbers 1

These people are assertive and always motivated as they have an inexhaustible source of energy. These individuals are perfect for professions where leadership skills are needed, such as managing contractors, ship captains, judges, prosecutors, freelance artists, politicians. Most importantly, these people cannot have bosses, they must be in control.

Favorable professions for numbers 2

These people are strong in spirit, but diplomats and mediators. They also could lecture and teach. Their best professions include teaching, counseling in schools, in any area of medicine, real estate sales, fashion designers, political advisors, and waiters.

Favorable professions for number 3

These people are very versatile, have a lot of enthusiasm when it comes to communicating and related jobs for them would be in the areas of the arts, writers, journalists, as broadcasters or even journalists, marketing, professions related to public relations, group therapies and pharmacists.

Favorable professions for numbers 4

These people are down to earth, hardworking, and would do super well in professions that require high levels of concentration. They would be super comfortable in administrative professions, banks, financial advisors, the stock market, engineering, architecture, and tour guides. They could be good lawyers and athletes as well.

Favorable professions for numbers 5

These people enjoy nature very much and are also good at risky professions. Suitable professions include public relations, sales, curator of antiques. Because they are prone to taking risks, they are often found in the military.

Favorable professions for number 6

These include Teaching and medicine Construction and engineering; carpentry and mechanics; and many jobs that are land-based. Here you can find people like Albert Einstein, the scientist who needs no introduction.

Favorable professions for numbers 7

These people are suitable for professions that require a high level of intelligence. These include professions such as mathematics, physics, chemistry. They are good military strategists, commercial business, theater arts, and film.

Favorable professions for numbers 8

These people have a lot of power of concentration, they are ambitious and courageous. Favorable professions would be policemen, car racers, surgeons, salesmen of pharmacy products and economic accountants.

Favorable professions for the number 9

These people favor professions that require diplomacy and fairness. They would be very effective as school counselors, councilors, politicians, pediatricians.

Favorable professions for 11

People with this number are complicated and difficult to understand. They have a strong desire to work but are not very tenacious. Suitable professions would be those that require a lot of knowledge, but do not necessarily require logical thinking but rather abstract thinking. Such jobs could be giving speeches, writing on philosophical subjects, political activists and advisors, technology, astrology, and psychic sciences.

Favorable professions for numbers 22

These people are unchanging and extensive in their thinking. They could group people and work together for the benefit of mankind. They are suitable for planning, organizing, diplomats, ambassadors, and presidents.

Birthday Number. Meaning

People with esoteric knowledge know that our soul chooses the day to be born into this world, and that we come with goals to achieve that are destined.

Your Birthday Number is the day you were born, and it has a very strong impact on your life. The Birthday Number identifies specific traits that will help you move forward in life.

By knowing your birthday number and its meaning, you can reduce or eliminate negative characteristics and refine positive ones.

How to Calculate Your Birthday Number

This is a simple calculation. You write the number on the date you were born and reduce it to a single digit if necessary. If you were born between the 1st and 9th of a month, you do not need to reduce the numbers. However, if your birthday was after the 10th of the month, you must reduce it until you reach a single digit.

Example:

If you were born on the 18th of the month, it would be 1 + 8 = 9.

Number of Birthdays 1

If you were born on the 1st, 10th, 19th or 28th of a month, your Birthday Number is 1.

This means that you have leadership skills and are very independent. You are creative and, you possess a lot of enthusiasm.

***If you were born on the 1st of the month**, you are charming and have creative ways to complete your goals. Almost every innovator or pioneer in history has had 1 as their Birthday Number.*

You possess easy earning skills and are dynamic by nature. At times you appear aloof and give the impression that you are ignoring others or are brusque.

As you are a natural leader, you rarely rest, your energy is nervous. Personally, when it comes to relationships you are strong. You are honest, have strong willpower and think quickly.

If you were born on the 10th of the month, *you are intuitive and are most successful when you listen to your hunches. You are dynamic, idealistic, and able to inspire others.*

You have a unique ability to reinvent yourself when necessary, and because you are so creative you can succeed in any business.

You don't like to pay attention to details and prefer to work alone. In your personal life you relate to many people, but you call few of them friends.

If you were born on the 19th of the month, *you are competitive, strong-willed, and like to succeed. You have an incredible ability to create and start new businesses and you like to take risks.*

Being a leader comes very naturally to you, but you work best when you are alone. Sometimes you may feel lonely, even when you are with a group of people and find it difficult to reflect on others.

Your personality is magnetic, and you prefer to overcome challenges in peace. You rarely get upset, but when it happens you explode, although you never hold grudges.

If you were born on the 28th of the month, *you are strong-willed, intelligent, and like to stand out. You* *are rebellious and do not like to follow rules as you are quite independent. You are very practical, but analytical and understand the basic concepts of humanity.*

You can apply logic to get the results you need. You are a perfectionist, but because you are innovative, you never fail.

Number of Birthdays 2

If you were born on the 2nd, 11th, 24th or 29th of the month, your Birthday Number is Number 2.

These people enjoy harmony and teamwork, but they are sensitive. They are very cooperative and enjoy the good things in life.

If you were born on the 2nd of the month*, you often play tricks with life and multitask with ease. Deep down, you want to be at peace, achieving balance in your life is one of your resolutions.*

You are diplomatic, have an ambitious side and like to work in a team. On an emotional level, you take things too seriously and can sometimes underestimate yourself.

Those who are close to you are important in your life, since, in your search for happiness, you need family and friends around you so you should try to choose your relationships carefully.

Your home is very important, you take care of it and love to spend time at home.

If you were born on the 11th of the month, *you are intuitive and enjoy hard work because this way you can transform your ideas into reality. You tend to be anxious; a balanced lifestyle is recommended for you.*

It is important that you get enough rest, as your energy levels can be depleted. You love being in contact with nature and surrounded by animals.

On an emotional level, you tend to get attached to the pain or disappointments of the past. You need to let go of the past, you need to work on your confidence levels so that you develop self-confidence.

If you were born on the 20th *of the month, you are tactful and diplomatic. You try to adapt in life and fit into any group because of your empathy and your ability to feel at ease wherever you are.*

You are happiest when you are with people who are like you, you are emotional and sensitive, and you sometimes overindulge those around you.

Other people take advantage of your desire to help, so it is important that you have quality time alone so you can enjoy peace.

If you were born on the 29th *of the month you are very sensitive, but you enjoy sharing time with others. You have a very strong character, but you easily inspire others.*

You have natural leadership abilities. If you wish to succeed in your profession, you must choose one that utilizes your talents. You tend to shyness, but you can overcome it, even if you are in the spotlight because your personality is very strong.

You like money and power, but you are very generous with others. It is very important for you to stay on the straight and narrow instead of opting for easy routes. You tend to mood swings, so you must keep your emotions in balance.

Inside you there are many feelings of insecurity, although you long to be able to love deeply. You are reserved, hiding your feelings for fear of being ridiculed. There is a possibility that in your childhood you may have had a trauma, and this may persuade you to have children.

Number of Birthdays 3

If you were born on the 3rd, 12th, 21st or 30th of the month, you have an incredible sense of humor and are very creative. You are a good communicator, kind, enthusiastic and like to have fun.

If you were born on the 3rd of the month, *you easily excel in your creative abilities. Your communication skills are excellent, and you are very popular.*

Other people are attracted to you in every way. Sometimes you seem distant because people don't always understand you, but there are even times when you don't understand yourself.

You possess the ability to keep your mood from deteriorating and are a problem solver par excellence.

If you were born on the 12th of the month, *you are a child in your heart and soul. As you are a people person, people are attracted to you, and you will always have friends. You have deep feelings and are committed to the people you love. You sometimes hide your feelings and your needs from others. This can lead you to be a mysterious person. You have a good vocabulary and express yourself well, which makes you a master, so you could be a public speaker. You have many interests in different areas of life, but it is* *important that you do not take on so many responsibilities.*

If you are born on the 21st of the month *you attract luck and opportunities. You enjoy sharing your good fortune with others. You are very popular but reserved at social events. You can talk to anyone about anything and have a natural optimism for life.*

Your attitude helps others improve their mood, and although you are stubborn at times, you have a curious mind. There are times when you feel nervous because you are constantly on the move; rest is important to you.

If you were born on the 30th of the month, *you are very creative and entertain others naturally. You are charming and succeed in life thanks to your creativity. Occasionally you find it difficult to achieve your personal goals. When you have money, you are generous, you are attracted to the good things in life. People find it difficult to get to know your true personality even though you are super fun to be with.*

Number of Birthdays 4

If your birthday is on the 4th, 13th, 22nd or 31st of the month, your Birthday Number is 4.

With this Birthday Number, you possess a desire for security and a need to create solid structures for your future. You are self-disciplined, sincere, and fair.

***If you were born on the 4th day of the month**, you are conventional and practical in your approach. You know how to get what you want in life and have the determination to do it.*

Sometimes your likes and dislikes are noticeable, and it is difficult for you to change your way of thinking. You are happy when you can enjoy life. It is important that you take time to increase your vitality. You should emphasize rest. In love it is very difficult for you to express your deepest emotions. You have appearances of seriousness, however, once people discover how kind you are, they adore you.

***If you were born on the 13th of the month**, you are a complex person. You are intellectual and have a monumental capacity for reasoning. You have a talent for overcoming obstacles and can sense when things are going wrong to counteract them.*

You are a good problem solver and are practical and energetic in your approach. Traditions are important to you, as is your family.

You have a balanced attitude, but sometimes, you allow yourself to have fun.

***If you were born on the 22nd of the month**, you are a natural organizer and leader. You are curious and seek answers to life's riddles. Although you are independent, you work well with groups.*

You have a natural zest for life, and balance is important to you. Your moods can easily wane. You possess many unusual friendships and have a need to make them happy. At times, you are sensitive and try to hide your feelings to project that you are strong.

***If you were born on the 31st of the month**, you are always on the move and travel frequently. You have artistic gifts, but your mind is strong and determined. You have ideas, and the ability to harness these ideas and put them into practice if necessary. You are hardworking, practical and have an anchor in the ground. You have high ideals and are honest. At times, you can be rigid in your ways, so try to be flexible.*

Number of Birthdays 5

If you were born on the 5th, 14th or 23rd of the month, your Birthday Number is 5.

You have an exacerbated sense of adventure. Being free is important to you, but this makes you impatient. You enjoy change, are resourceful, curious, and an advanced thinker.

__If you were born on the 5th of the month,__ you are untraditional, and you like to do whatever you want. You have a unique outlook on life. Your energy is boundless, this means that you are in constant motion and can be rebellious because you hate to follow the rules. Your personality is magnetic, others find you fascinating. You have difficulty with commitment and are quick to analyze.

__If you were born on the 14th of the month__, you enjoy calculated risks, and this is part of your personality. You possess an excellent memory, which leads you to think about the pains of the past. You need to be flexible and adaptable. You enjoy food and drink; you indulge your senses too much. You are very generous, and others adore you.

__If you were born on the 23rd of the month__, you are versatile and think very fast. You trust your intuition; you may have psychic abilities. You always listen to your inner voice, you possess a lot of energy, and this *can unsettle you and lead you to experience new things. Although you face many challenges, you always land on your feet.*

Number of Birthdays 6

If your birthday falls on the 6th, 15th or 24th, your Birthday Number will be 6.

You avoid arguments, preferring peace, and harmony in your environment. You often feel uneasy if you argue with others. People are attracted to your magnetism.

If you were born on the 6th of the month, *you have business skills, you are artistic and charming. You can overcome any challenge. You give importance to your family life and always help those in need. You often take on too much responsibility.*

You enjoy giving advice to others but find it difficult to accept criticism.

If you were born on the 15th of the month, *you are sensitive. You are empathetic and will try to help those in need. Sometimes you take on other people's problems and it can be very difficult for you to let them go. Family life is very important to you. You are very respected in business; you attract influential people into your life.*

***If you were born on the 24th of the month**, you work hard to achieve your goals, and you like to be simple. The key to your success is your practical and fair approach. You often take over when others can't keep up, but you expect others to take responsibility as well. You often find yourself surrounded by children, or by people with a jovial nature. Your home is your sanctuary and music are your favorite way to relax.*

Number of Birthdays 7

If you were born on the 7th, 16th and 25th of the month, your Birthday Number is 7.

You are reflective and are always looking for meaning in life. You take a measured approach when you must make decisions because you hate to make mistakes. You are attracted to nature because it nurtures your mind and soul.

***If you were born on the 7th of the month**, you have a distant appearance, because you possess a natural shyness. You love privacy and few people know the real you. You are very curious and are constantly asking questions, although you are reluctant to be questioned. You trust your intuition.*

***If you were born on the 16th of the month**, your power of perception is excellent, you detect evil immediately. It is important that you finish what you started, for that you must be more analytical. You are often considered a perfectionist. You must try to see the positive aspects of life, as you must control your mood swings.*

***If you were born on the 25th of the month**, you have a need for tranquility and long to be alone. It is important for you to be able to relax and revitalize your mind. You are attracted to the sea, you are very curious, and you are always trying to discover how things work. It is important that you follow your instincts and gain metaphysical knowledge.*

Number of Birthdays 8

If you were born on the 8th, 17th or 26th of the month, your Birthday Number will be 8.

You have a need to be your own boss or, be in a position where you have responsibilities and can supervise others. You are highly motivated by material possessions. You are very confident and ambitious.

***If you were born on the 8th of the month**, you have an incredible magnetic aura around you. Some people* *find you intimidating. You like to make your own decisions and hate being told what to do.*

Success is very important in your life, and you find happiness in having money and when you strive for material success.

***If you were born on the 17th of the month**, you are ambitious and successful in any business. You have a good memory, but also addictive tendencies. You are sometimes self-centered. You are analytical and need concrete evidence, rather than listening to random information. You are organized and succeed in finance.*

***If you were born on the 26th of the month**, you possess an innate need for balanced relationships. You appreciate your home and family but are almost always too busy to enjoy them. You are happiest when surrounded by animals. You have leadership skills, are organized, but suffer from stress. It is important that you learn to stay calm and manage stressors.*

Number of Birthdays 9

***If you were born on the 9th, 18th or 27th of the month**, your Birthday Number is 9.*

You have a desire to make the world a better place. You are broad-minded and interested in world political issues. You can understand people with different types of thoughts.

If you were born on the 9th of the month, your heart is kind and compassionate. You are idealistic and will always reach out to those in need. You are reserved with your personal life, and very creative. You are sociable and easily attracted. You are a dreamer and strive to inspire others. Remember to take care of your health.

***If you were born on the 18th of the month**, you have the potential to be successful. You are artistic, know your strengths, are very independent and a leader. Your tastes are refined, and you need to keep yourself mentally stimulated. You tend to be disinterested in worldly things.*

***If you were born on the 27th of the month**, you are very private with your personal life and keep your emotions to yourself. You are a passionate advocate for those around you and your communication skills are incredible. You have a lot of creativity; you could be a very good writer or composer. You could also be interested in politics.*

About the Authors

In addition to her astrological knowledge, Rubi has an abundant professional education; she holds certifications in Psychology, Hypnosis, Reiki, Bioenergetic Crystal Healing, Angelic Healing, Dream Interpretation and is a Spiritual Instructor. Rubi has knowledge of Gemology, which she uses to program stones or minerals and turn them into powerful Amulets or Talismans of protection.

Rubi has a practical and results-oriented character, which has allowed her to have a special and integrative vision of several worlds, facilitating solutions to specific problems. Alina writes the Monthly Horoscopes for the website of the American Association of Astrologers; you can read them at www.astrologers.com. At this moment she writes a weekly column in El Nuevo Herald newspaper on spiritual topics, published every Monday in digital and printed form. He also has a program and the weekly Horoscope on the YouTube channel of this newspaper.

Her Astrological Yearbook is published every year in the newspaper "Diario las Américas", under the column Rubi Astrologa.

Rubi has written several articles on astrology for the monthly publication "Today's Astrologer", has taught classes on Astrology, Tarot, Palm Reading, Crystal Healing, and Esotericism. She has weekly videos on esoteric topics on her YouTube channel: Rubi Astrologa. She had her own Astrology show broadcasted daily through Flamingo T.V., has been interviewed by several T.V. and radio programs, and every year she publishes her "Astrological Yearbook" with the horoscope sign by sign, and other interesting mystical topics.

She is the author of the books "Rice and Beans for the Soul" Part I, II, and III, a compilation of esoteric articles, published in English, Spanish, French, Italian and Portuguese. "Money for All Pockets", "Love for All Hearts", "Health for All Bodies", Astrological Yearbook 2021, Horoscope 2022, Rituals and Spells for Success in 2022, Spells and Secrets, Astrology Classes, Rituals and Charms 2024 and Chinese Horoscope 2024 are all available in five languages: English, Italian, French, Japanese and German.

Rubi speaks English and Spanish perfectly, combining all her talents and knowledge in her readings. She currently resides in Miami, Florida.

*For more information you can visit **the website** www.esoterismomagia.com*

Alina A. Rubi is the daughter of Alina Rubi. She is currently studying psychology at Florida International University.

Since she was a child, she has been interested in all metaphysical and esoteric subjects and has practiced astrology and Kabbalah since she was four years old. She has knowledge of Tarot, Reiki, and Gemology. She is not only the author, but also the editor, along with her sister Angeline A. Rubi, of all the books published by her and her mother.

*For further information please contact them by email: **rubiediciones29@gmail.com***

Bibliography

Articles published by one of the authors in the Nuevo Herald.